We Learn About™ Mass

Second Edition

Text by **Gerard Moore**

Cover art by **Jim Burrows**
Interior illustrations by **Dorothy Woodward, RSJ**

LTP

LITURGY
TRAINING
PUBLICATIONS

Nihil Obstat
Very Reverend Daniel A. Smilanic, JCD
Vicar for Canonical Services
Archdiocese of Chicago
May 5, 2011

Imprimatur
Reverend Monsignor John F. Canary, STL, DMIN
Vicar General
Archdiocese of Chicago
May 5, 2011

We Learn About™ Mass was first published in 2007 by St Pauls Publications, Strathfield, Australia. Copyright © Gerard Moore, 2007; illustrations © Dorothy Woodward, RSJ, 2007.

Excerpts from the English translation of *The Roman Missal* © 2010, International Commission on English in the Liturgy Corporation (ICEL). All rights reserved.

WE LEARN ABOUT™ MASS, SECOND EDITION © 2011 Archdiocese of Chicago: Liturgy Training Publications, 3949 South Racine Avenue, Chicago IL 60609; 1-800-933-1800, fax 1-800-933-7094, e-mail: orders@ltp.org. All rights reserved. See our website at www.LTP.org.

Cover art by Jim Burrows
Interior illustrations by Dorothy Woodward, RSJ

Printed in the United States of America.

20 19 18 17 16   3 4 5 6 7

ISBN: 978-1-61671-034-7

EWLAM2

Presented by
Catholic Daughters
Of
The Americas

Court Bishop Edward Celestin Daly, O.P.
No. 1945
Ankeny, Iowa

My name is _____

The name of my parish is _____

The name of my school is _____

Table of Contents

Introduction   vii

① Introductory Rites   1
The Sign of the Cross   4
The Greeting   4
The Penitential Act   5
The Gloria   6
The Collect   8

② The Liturgy of the Word   9
The First Reading, Psalm, and Second Reading   10
The Gospel   11
The Homily   12
The Profession of Faith   12
Prayer of the Faithful   15

③ The Liturgy of the Eucharist   17
The Presentation and Preparation of the Gifts   17
The Eucharistic Prayer   20
The Preface Dialogue   21
The Holy, Holy, Holy   22
Memorial Acclamation   23
The Doxology (Amen)   24
The Lord's Prayer   25
Sign of Peace   26
Lamb of God   27
Communion   28
Prayer after Communion   30

④ Concluding Rites   31
The Blessing   31
Final Dismissal   34

⑤ Answer Key   35

Introduction

The celebration of Mass, which is also called the celebration of Eucharist, is very important.

We come to Mass to praise God and give thanks for all of the blessings we have received. At Mass we are nourished by God's word and by Eucharist. During Mass we pray for ourselves and all the needs of our world. We leave Mass with renewed energy to love our brothers and sisters.

At Mass we are all participants: there is no place for spectators! The participation of everyone is important. We all have our specific roles. We dialogue with the priest and pray aloud with the whole congregation. We participate by listening attentively as the Word of God is read aloud and explained. In Holy Communion we eat and drink of the Body and Blood of Christ. We sing psalms, and hymns, and chants. Some of us minister as readers, as singers; others may take part in the procession of gifts or help as altar servers. Some may assist the priest and deacon to distribute Holy Communion.

This book has been written to help you understand more about Mass, and how you participate in it. You will learn the prayers and responses you say out loud, when to stand, to sit, and to kneel, and some of the other actions that are part of Mass.

Introductory Rites

The Sunday Mass begins with a number of steps.

The first step occurs when we enter the church, gathering together as Christ's sisters and brothers. From the time we leave home we should be preparing our minds and hearts to come together to meet the Lord.

Draw a picture of yourself leaving home to come to Mass.

ACTIVITY:

What is the best way to prepare for Mass once we have entered the church?

(Write your answer below, and share it with others.)

The second step is when the priest and ministers enter in a procession. There is always a cross. Usually there are candles. Sometimes there is a minister carrying the Book of the Gospels, and at other times incense.

The ministers enter the sanctuary at the front of the church, and the priest and deacon kiss the altar out of respect. Sometimes they incense the altar and the cross. During the procession we all stand and sing the Entrance Chant. Singing unites us and helps us enter into the Mass.

The Sign of the Cross

The priest makes the Sign of the Cross.

He says: *In the name of the* _____ ,
and of the _____ *, and of the* _____
_____ .

We respond: *A* _____ .

ACTIVITY:

Practice the way we make the Sign of the Cross.

The Greeting

The priest greets us all:

He says: *The Lord be with you.*

We respond: *And* _____ *your* _____ .

Usually on Sunday the priest says a few words of welcome.

4

The Penitential Act

After the Greeting, the priest invites us to make the Penitential Act. This can take different forms.

- One is to pray the prayer called the Confiteor.

    I confess to almighty God,
    and to you, my brothers and sisters,
    that I have greatly sinned,
    in my thoughts and in my words,
    in what I have done, and what I have failed to do,

    And, striking the breast, they say:

    through my fault, through my fault,
    through my most grievous fault;
    therefore I ask blessed Mary, ever-Virgin,
    all the Angels and Saints,
    and you, my brothers and sisters,
    to pray for me to the Lord our God.

- The second option is a call and response between the priest and the assembly.

    The priest says: Have mercy on us, O Lord.

    We respond: *For we have sinned against you.*

    Then the priest says: Show us O Lord, your mercy.

    We respond: *And grant us your salvation.*

- Another way is to make petitions, usually led by the priest.

When the priest or minister sings or says, "Lord, have mercy," we respond with "Lord, have mercy." When the priest or minister sings or says, "Christ, have mercy," we respond with " _____ , _____ _____ ."

• On Sundays, especially during Easter Time, the priest may bless some water and sprinkle us, reminding us of our Baptism.

The Gloria

The Gloria is a song. As we sing it, our hearts are filled with praise for God. Sometimes the text is said rather than sung. We do not sing or recite the Gloria in Advent or Lent.

Glory to God in the highest,
    and on earth peace to people
        of good will.

We praise you,
we bless you,
we adore you,
we glorify you,
we give you thanks for your great glory,
Lord God, heavenly King,
O God, almighty Father.

6

Lord Jesus Christ, Only Begotten Son,
Lord God, Lamb of God, Son of the Father,
you take away the sins of the world,
    have mercy on us;
you take away the sins of the world,
    receive our prayer;
you are seated at the right hand of the Father,
    have mercy on us.

For you alone are the Holy One,
you alone are the Lord,
you alone are the Most High,
Jesus Christ,
with the Holy Spirit,
in the glory of God the Father.
Amen.

ACTIVITIES:

1. Read the Gloria and underline the lines that you find the most interesting.

2. Learn to sing the Gloria.

3. Find out why we don't pray the Gloria in Advent or Lent.

The Collect

The Collect is led by the priest.
He invites us to reflect for a short time when he says: *Let us pray.*

After our silent reflection, he then prays the prayer.

We respond by saying: *A_____.*

②

The Liturgy of the Word

At the end of the Collect we sit and prepare to hear the Word of the Lord.

On Sundays we listen to three readings and a psalm, all taken from the Bible. Christ himself is present and speaks to us in the readings, and the Holy Spirit moves in our hearts as we listen attentively. After the readings we listen to the homily, pray the Profession of Faith, and make our petitions in the Universal Prayer or Prayer of the Faithful. The readings are in a book called the _____.

The First Reading

The First Reading is usually taken from the Old Testament (during Easter the First Reading is from the Acts of the Apostles, which is from the New Testament). We hear some of the great stories and sayings about God's love for the world and for us.

The reading finishes when the reader says: *The word of the Lord.*

We reply: _____ _____
_____ _____ .

The Responsorial Psalm

After the reading we have a short silence, and then we sing the psalm. The psalms are holy songs from the Bible. They can be sung in many different ways. Often we are invited to sing the response, although sometimes we say it together.

The Second Reading

Our next reading comes from the New Testament.

Again, the reading finishes when the reader says:

_____ _____ _____ _____ _____ .

And we reply: *Thanks be to God.*

The Gospel

It is now time for the Gospel. These special readings are taken from four writers, called evangelists. The names of the four evangelists are _____ , _____ , _____ , and _____ .

We know the Gospel is special because we often sing the word A_____ before it starts. And, we stand rather than sit. We also know it is special because we sometimes include the Gospel in a book called the _____ _____ _____ _____ . We process with this book and encircle it with candles. We incense it and we hold it high.

The person who reads the Gospel is either a deacon or a priest.

The Gospel begins with a dialogue:

> Deacon or priest: *The Lord be with you.*
>
> We respond: *And with your spirit.*
>
> Deacon or priest: *A reading from the holy Gospel according to*
>
> _____ .
>
> We respond: _____ _____ _____ _____ , _____ .

After the reading is finished the priest says:
The Gospel of the Lord.

We reply: _____ _____ _____ ,

_____ _____ _____ .

The Homily

In the homily the priest or
deacon helps us understand the
meanings of the Bible readings
and the lessons they can teach
us for our lives. We sit during
the homily to help us listen
more attentively.

The Profession of Faith

This prayer is also known as the Creed. It is sung or recited on
Sundays and special days, and it involves all the people. We
stand for the Profession of Faith. It is important to try to learn it.

> I believe in one God,
> > the Father almighty,
> > maker of heaven and earth,
> > of all things visible and invisible.

> I believe in one Lord Jesus Christ,
> > the Only Begotten Son of God,
> > born of the Father before all ages.
> > God from God, Light from Light,
> > true God from true God,
> > begotten, not made,
> > > consubstantial with the Father;
> > through him all things were made.

For us men and for our salvation
he came down from heaven,

[at this time , we bow]

and by the Holy Spirit was incarnate
of the Virgin Mary,
and became man.

[at this time we stand upright]

For our sake he was crucified under Pontius Pilate,
he suffered death and was buried,
and rose again on the third day
in accordance with the Scriptures.
He ascended into heaven
and is seated at the right hand of the Father.
He will come again in glory
to judge the living and the dead,
and his kingdom will have no end.

I believe in the Holy Spirit, the Lord, the giver of life,
who proceeds from the Father and the Son,
who with the Father and the Son is adored and glorified,
who has spoken through the Prophets.

I believe in one, holy, catholic and apostolic Church.
I confess one Baptsim for the forgiveness of sins
and I look forward to the resurrection of the dead
and the life of the world to come. Amen.

We may also say a shorter form of the Creed. This creed is called the Apostles' Creed. We also say this prayer when we pray the Rosary.

I believe in God,
the Father almighty,
Creator of heaven and earth,
and in Jesus Christ, his only Son, our Lord,

[Bow until after the words "Virgin Mary."]

who was conceived by the Holy Spirit,
born of the Virgin Mary,
suffered under Pontius Pilate,
was crucified, died and was buried;
he descended into hell;
on the third day he rose again from the dead;
he ascended into heaven,
and is seated at the right
    hand of God the Father almighty;
from there he will come to judge the living and the dead.

I believe in the Holy Spirit,
the holy catholic Church,
the communion of saints,
the forgiveness of sins,
the resurrection of the body,
and life everlasting. Amen.

Prayer of the Faithful

In the readings we have heard what God has done for us. As we remain standing we now ask God to look after everyone and everything in creation.

We usually ask God to watch over four areas.

- We ask God to help the Church be strong and faithful.

- We ask God to encourage and advise our local, national, and world leaders.

- We ask God to look after anyone who is in need, such as the hungry, the sick, the cold, and those without homes.

- We ask God for the things we need in our own community and family.

These prayers are truly our prayers—the Church, those who have been baptized—and each one is led by a person from the congregation or the deacon.

ACTIVITY:

Write a prayer for each of these four areas.

1. _____
   _____
   _____
   _____
   _____
   _____

2. _____
   _____
   _____
   _____
   _____

3. _____
   _____
   _____
   _____
   _____

4. _____
   _____
   _____
   _____
   _____

③

The Liturgy
of the Eucharist

This part of Mass has three stages. The first is when we prepare the gifts of bread and wine. The second is when the great prayer of thanksgiving is prayed. The third stage is when we receive Holy Communion.

Presentation and Preparation of the Gifts

We bring forward to the priest the bread and wine that will be consecrated in the great prayer of thanksgiving. We may also bring some water. During the procession the people sit.

As the gifts are brought forward we may sing.

The bread will become our food and the wine will become our drink. They are the food and drink of heaven blessed by God and shared by him with us.

ACTIVITY:

What are some of the different meanings we give to the words *bread* and *wine*? For instance, bread can signify food. What are some others?

Bread can signify   Wine can signify

_____   _____

_____   _____

_____   _____

Because all good things come from God, we too are encouraged to be generous. Sometimes during the Presentation and Preparation of the Gifts, money and gifts are collected for the poor and the needs of the Church.

Holding the bread, the priest prays:
> Blessed are you, Lord God of all creation,
> for through your goodness we have received
> the bread we offer you:
> fruit of the earth and work of human hands,
> it will become for us the bread of life.

We respond: _____ _____ _____

_____ _____ .

Holding the cup of wine, the priest prays a similar prayer:

> *Blessed are you, Lord God of all creation,*
> *for through your goodness we have received*
> *the wine we offer you:*
> *fruit of the vine and work of human hands,*
> *it will become our spiritual drink.*

We respond: _____ _____ _____

_____ _____ .

The priest leads us as we ask God to accept our gifts:

> Priest: *Pray, brothers and sisters,*
> *that my sacrifice and yours*
> *may be acceptable to God,*
> *the almighty Father.*

> We respond: *May the Lord accept the sacrifice*
> *at your hands*
> *for the praise and glory of his name,*
> *for our good*
> *and the good of all his holy Church.*

At this stage we stand up and the priest prays the Prayer over the Gifts.

We respond by praying: *A* _____ .

The Eucharistic Prayer

The word *Eucharist* means "thanksgiving." It comes from the Greek language.

This is the great prayer in Mass. During this prayer we give thanks to God for creating the world, for making us, and for watching over us. Especially we praise and thank God for sending us Christ who showed us how to live. We do not forget God's other gift, the gift of the Holy Spirit who continually is with us and opens our eyes to grace and peace.

```
┌─────────────────────────────────────────────────────┐
│                    ACTIVITY:                          │
│                                                       │
│  Complete this sentence:                              │
│  Some of the things I am thankful for are             │
│  _____     │
│  _____     │
│  _____     │
│  _____     │
│                                                       │
└─────────────────────────────────────────────────────┘
```

In the Eucharistic Prayer we call upon God the Father through the Holy Spirit to bless the bread and wine to become the Body and Blood of Christ. When we eat and drink the consecrated bread and wine at Holy Communion we are united with Christ, the Son of God and our brother.

The prayer has many parts.

The Preface Dialogue

Still standing, we begin together like this:

Priest: *The Lord be with you.*

We respond: *And with your spirit.*

Priest: *Lift up your hearts.*

We respond: *We lift them up to the Lord.*

Priest: *Let us give thanks to the Lord our God.*

We respond: *It is right and just.*

Then the priest continues the prayer by praising the things that God has done for us and for creation.

The Holy, Holy, Holy (the Sanctus)

All together we respond with a song of praise:

> Holy, Holy, Holy Lord God of hosts.
> Heaven and earth are full of your glory.
> Hosanna in the highest.
> Blessed is he who comes in the name of the Lord.
> Hosanna in the highest.

In this acclamation we are united with the angels and all creation.

ACTIVITY:

Learn to sing the Holy, Holy, Holy. Use the musical setting your parish church uses.

After this acclamation we kneel. The priest then continues the Eucharistic Prayer. During this part of the prayer he invites the Holy Spirit to bless the bread and the wine, which become the Body and Blood of Christ. He does this because this is what Jesus asked us to do to remember him. He becomes present to us, and in Holy Communion is united with us. Jesus also invites the Holy Spirit to bless us, so that we will become more like him.

As the prayer continues, we hear the priest recall the words and actions of Jesus at the Last Supper when he gave us Eucharist and asked us to continue it as a memorial of him.

Memorial Acclamation

During the Eucharistic Prayer we praise God out loud and all together with an acclamation.

The priest leads us: *The mystery of faith.*

We have three ways of praising God:

We proclaim your _____ , O Lord,
and profess your _____
until you come _____ .

or

When we eat this _____ *and* _____
        this Cup,
we _____ *your Death, O Lord,*
until you come again.

or

Save us, Savior of the _____ ,
for by your Cross and _____ ,
you have set us free.

The priest then continues with the prayer, asking God to grant our requests.

The Doxology (Amen)

The Eucharistic Prayer ends with a great act of praise. The priest and deacon hold high the consecrated bread and wine, and give glory to God:

> Through him, and with him, and in him,
> O God almighty Father,
> in the unity of the Holy Spirit,
> all glory and honor is yours,
> for ever and ever.

We bring the prayer to an end when we sing:
A _____ .

We now stand.

The Lord's Prayer

As the time for Holy Communion comes closer we make special preparation. We pray the prayer that Jesus himself taught us. This prayer, the Our Father, reminds us that God gives us our bread each day.

Priest and people all pray together:

> Our Father, who art in heaven,
> hallowed be thy name;
> thy kingdom come;
> thy will be done on earth as it is in heaven.
> Give us this day our daily bread;
> and forgive us our trespasses
> as we forgive those who trespass against us;
> and lead us not into temptation,
> but deliver us from evil.

After the Lord's Prayer, the priest prays:

Deliver us, Lord, we pray, from every evil,
graciously grant peace in our days,
that, by the help of your mercy,
we may be always free from sin
and safe from all distress,
as we await the blessed hope
and the coming of our Savior, Jesus Christ.

We respond: *For the kingdom,*
the _____ *and* _____
_____ *are yours,*
_____ *and* _____ _____ .

Sign of Peace

Part of our preparation for Holy Communion is to receive the gift of peace that Christ gives us.

The priest says:
Lord Jesus Christ,
who said to your Apostles:
Peace, I leave you, my peace I give you;
look not on our sins,
but on the faith of your Church,
and graciously grant her peace and unity
in accordance with your will.

Who live and reign for ever and ever.

We respond: _____ .

The priest says: *The peace of the Lord be with you always.*

We reply: _____ _____

_____ _____ .

The deacon or priest says: *Let us offer each other the sign of peace.*

We now receive this gift from our neighbor and offer this same peace to all around us. We do this by shaking _____ and saying, "Peace be _____ _____"
to those who are near us.

ACTIVITY:

Do you know of other forms of greeting that people use across the world? (For instance, in Korea people bow to one another.)

_____

_____

_____

_____

Lamb of God (Fraction of the Bread)

The priest breaks the consecrated bread and pours the consecrated wine so that we can receive Holy Communion. It is a sign that we all eat the same food together and are like one family united together. Jesus broke the bread at the Last Supper.

During the breaking of the bread we sing or say:

> Lamb of God, you take away the sins of the world,
>   have mercy on us.
> Lamb of God, you take away the sins of the world,
>   have mercy on us.
> Lamb of God, you take away the sins of the world,
>   grant us peace.

At the end of the Lamb of God we kneel.

Communion

The priest now invites us to come to the Lord's table and receive Holy Communion.

> The priest says: *Behold the Lamb of God,*
> *behold him who takes away the sins of the world.*
> *Blessed are those called to the supper of the Lamb.*
>
> We respond together with the priest:
> *Lord, I am not*
>
> _____
>
> that you should enter under my roof,
> *but only* _____ _____ _____
> and my soul shall be healed.

ACTIVITY:

Read from the Gospel according to Matthew (8:3–13) to see where these words come from and who said them.

After we have said these words, we join in the procession, singing joyfully as we go forward to the altar to receive the Body and Blood of Christ.

The minister of Holy Communion is the priest but it can also be the deacon or another member of the congregation.

The minister holds the Body of Christ before us and says: *The Body of Christ.*

We respond: *A* _____ , and then we eat the host.

Another minister may give us the cup to drink, saying: *The Blood of Christ.*

Again we reply, *A* _____ .

We then return to our place, singing still, and when we are at our seat we pray silently and specially with Jesus in our hearts.

ACTIVITY:

Write a prayer to Jesus.

Dear Jesus, _____

_____

_____

_____

Prayer after Communion

After the procession to receive Holy Communion has finished and the singing has ended, we pray the Prayer after Communion. This prayer begins when the priest says: *Let us pray.*

At this signal we all stand, and after a short silence the priest then prays the prayer.

We respond: *A* _____ .

Concluding Rites

The Mass now comes to a close and we prepare to leave the church. We have been refreshed and are now keen to live like sisters and brothers of Christ, following his example and living his teachings.

The Blessing

After any announcements the priest gives a blessing.

> Priest: *The Lord be with you.*

We respond: _____ _____

_____ _____ .

> Priest: *May almighty God bless you,*
> *the Father, and the Son,*
> *and the Holy Spirit.*

We respond: *A* _____ .

Sometimes, on special days like Easter Sunday, the priest may give a longer and more solemn blessing. Here is an example.

> Priest: *The Lord be with you.*

We respond: _____ _____

_____ _____ .

Priest: *May God, who by the Resurrection of his*
        Only Begotten Son
        was pleased to confer on you
        the gift of redemption and of adoption,
        give you gladness by his blessing.

We respond: *A _____ .*

Priest: *May he, by whose redeeming work*
        you have received the gift of everlasting
        freedom,
        make you heirs to an eternal inheiritance.

We respond: *A _____ .*

Priest: *And may you, who have already risen*
        with Christ
        in Baptism through faith,
        by living in a right manner on this earth,
        be united with him in the homeland
        of heaven.

We respond: *A _____ .*

Priest: *And may the blessing of almighty God,*
        the Father, and the Son, and the
        Holy Spirit,
        come down on you and remain
        with you for ever.

We respond: *A _____ .*

As the priest gives the blessing, we follow the custom and make the Sign of the Cross.

ACTIVITY:

When Mass has finished, what are some of the things I can do to share the love I have received from Jesus?

(Write your answers below, and share them with others.)

Final Dismissal

The deacon or priest leads the final prayer: He may say one of
the four options:

> *Go forth the Mass is ended.*
> *Go and announce the Gospel of the Lord.*
> *Go in peace, glorifying the Lord by*
> *your life.*
> *Go in peace.*

We respond: _____ _____ _____ _____ .

The Mass is now finished, and we sometimes have a song and
a procession to bring everything to a close. As we leave we
begin again to live as Jesus taught us, especially to bring love
and peace to everyone we meet.

Answer Key

You have written down a number of prayers and Mass responses in this book. Check below to see if you have written them in correctly. The words you had to write are printed in bold letters.

Chapter 1: Introductory Rites

Page 4: The Sign of the Cross

> In the name of the **Father**, and of the **Son**, and of the **Holy Spirit.**
>
> We respond: **Amen.**

Page 4: The Greeting

> We respond: And **with** your **spirit.**

Page 6: The Penitential Act

> We respond with **Christ, have mercy.**

Page 8: The Collect

> We respond by saying: **Amen.**

Chapter 2: The Liturgy of the Word

Page 9: The Liturgy of the Word

- The readings are in a book called the **Lectionary.**

Page 10: The First Reading

We reply: **Thanks be to God.**

Page 10: The Second Reading

Again the reading finishes when the reader says:
The word of the Lord.

Page 11: The Gospel

The names of the four evangelists are **Matthew, Mark, Luke,** and **John.**

We know the Gospel is special because we often sing the word **Alleluia**.

We also know it is special because we sometimes include the Gospel in a book called the **Book of the Gospels.**

Deacon or priest: A reading from the holy Gospel according to **Matthew** or **Mark** or **Luke** or **John.**

We respond: **Glory to you, O Lord.**

Page 12: The Gospel

We reply: **Praise to you, Lord Jesus Christ.**

Chapter 3: The Liturgy of the Eucharist

Page 18: The Presentation and Preparation of the Gifts

We respond: **Blessed be God for ever.**

Page 19: The Presentation and Preparation of the Gifts

We respond: **Blessed be God for ever.**

We respond by saying: **Amen.**

Page 23: Memorial Acclamation

We proclaim your **Death**, O Lord,

and profess your **Resurrection**

until you come **again**.

or

When we **eat** this Bread and **drink** this Cup,

we **proclaim** your Death, O Lord,

until you come again.

or

Save us, Savior of the **world**,

for by your Cross and **Resurrection**,

you have set us free.

Page 24: The Doxology (Amen)

We bring the prayer to an end when we sing: **Amen**.

Page 25: The Lord's Prayer

We respond: For the kingdom, the **power**, and **the glory** are yours, **now** and **for ever**.

Page 26: Sign of Peace

We respond: **Amen**.

We reply: **And with your spirit**.

We do this by shaking **hands** and saying, "Peace be **with you**" to those who are near us.

Page 28: Communion

We respond together with the priest: Lord, I am not **worthy**

that you should enter under my roof,

but only **say the word**

and my soul shall be healed.

Page 29: Communion

We respond: **Amen**.

Again we reply: **Amen**.

Page 30: Prayer after Communion

We respond: **Amen**.

Chapter 4: Concluding Rites

Page 31: The Blessing

We respond: **And with your spirit.**

We respond: **Amen.**

We respond: **And with your spirit.**

We respond: **Amen.**

Page 32: The Blessing

We respond: **Amen.**

We respond: **Amen.**

We respond: **Amen.**

Page 34: Final Dismissal

We respond: **Thanks be to God.**

The Author

Dr. Gerard Moore has taught liturgy for many years, and has served as a consultant to the International Commission on English in the Liturgy. He is currently the Director of Research for the Sydney College of Divinity.

The Illustrators

Jim Burrows provided the cover art. Jim shares the Good News of the Gospel through a variety of media. He creates a weekly Lectionary-based cartoon series for church bulletins and diocesan newspapers. Jim is enrolled in the master's degree program in pastoral studies at Loyola University New Orleans and is in formation for the permanent diaconate for the Diocese of Monterey. He is a certified catechist at Mission San Luis Obispo in California.

Dorothy Woodward, RSJ, is responsible for the interior art. She has wide experience in Catholic education, and a special interest in liturgical art and design.

Resources

To learn more about the Mass, visit www.LTP.org for an array of resources for children, parents, teachers, and parishes.